Contents

Words that appear in **bold** are explained in the glossary on page 46.

Continents and Oceans

The land on the Earth's surface is divided into seven areas called **continents**. The seven continents in the world are Europe, Asia, Africa, North and South America, Australia and Antarctica.

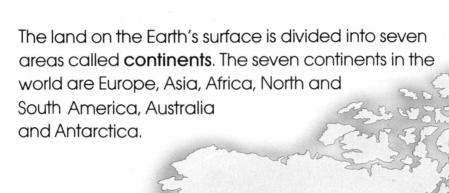

ARCTIC OCEAN

NORTH AMERICA

ATLANTIC OCEAN

PACIFIC OCEAN

SOUTH AMERICA

FACTS

Highest mountain in the world:
Mt Everest, Asia. 8,848m
Largest lake in the world:
Caspian Sea, Asia.
438,695 sq km
Longest river in the world:
River Nile, Africa. 6,670 km

N
W E
S

The Puffin
Picture
Atlas
of the World

Julie Warne and John Lace

Mapwork by Peter Bull   Illustrated by Robert Wheeler

PUFFIN BOOKS

in association with Wayland (Publishers) Ltd

Key

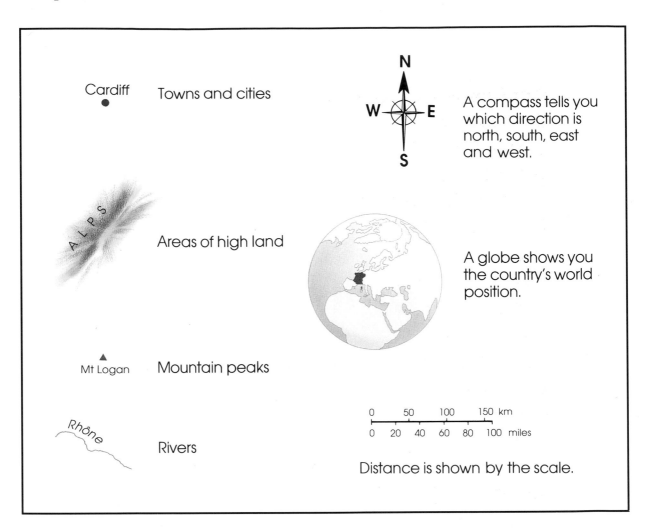

Cardiff
●

Towns and cities

N
W ✦ **E**
S

A compass tells you which direction is north, south, east and west.

A L P S

Areas of high land

A globe shows you the country's world position.

▲
Mt Logan

Mountain peaks

| 0 | 50 | 100 | 150 km |
| 0 | 20 | 40 | 60 | 80 | 100 miles |

Rhône

Rivers

Distance is shown by the scale.

PUFFIN BOOKS

Published by the Penguin Group
Penguin Books Ltd, 27 Wrights Lane, London W8 5TZ, England
Penguin Books USA Inc., 375 Hudson Street, New York, New York 10014, USA
Penguin Books Australia Ltd, Ringwood, Victoria, Australia
Penguin Books Canada Ltd, 10 Alcorn Avenue, Toronto, Ontario, Canada M4V 3B2
Penguin Books (NZ) Ltd, 182-190 Wairau Road, Auckland 10, New Zealand

Penguin Books Ltd, Registered Offices: Harmondsworth, Middlesex, England

First published by Wayland (Publishers) Ltd 1992
Published in Puffin Books 1993
10 9 8 7 6 5 4 3 2 1

Copyright © Wayland (Publishers) Ltd, 1992
All rights reserved

The moral rights of the author and illustrator have been asserted

Filmset in Avant Garde

Printed and bound by G. Canale and C.S.p.A., Turin, Italy

Title page photograph: The world from space.

Picture acknowledgements
The publishers would like to thank the following for allowing their photographs to be reproduced in this book: Bryan and Cherry Alexander 44 (above); Bruce Coleman Ltd 6 (Wedigo Ferchland), 8 below (Dieter and Mary Plage), 9 right (O. Langrand), 12 middle (Geoff Dore), 14 above (Michael Klinec), 14 below (Herbert Kranawetter), 16 top left (Francisco Marquez), 19 below (Jessica Ehlers), 25 above (Nicholas Devore), 25 below (Michael Freeman), 28 above (John Cancalosi), 29 below (Steven Kaufman), 30 below (L. C. Marigo), 31 (Dr Eckart Pott), 32 above (Peter Davey); Ecoscene 8 top right, 21 top (Corbett), 32 below (Gryniewicz); Eye Ubiquitous *front cover* top left (P. Thomson), top right (Nick Wiseman), bottom left (M. McKee), 8 top left (M. W. Powles), 9 left, 15 (Paul Prestidge), 18 (David Cumming), 22 above (Frank Leather), 23 below (Julia Waterlow), 27 below (L. Fordyce), 33 below; Liz Miller 8 top right; Francesca Motisi 33 above; Tony Stone Worldwide *title page*, 7; Wayland Picture Library *front cover* bottom right, 11 (both), 12 (above and below), 13, 16 (above right and below), 17, 24, 27 (above), 28 (left and below), 29 (both top), 30 (three above), 34, 35 (both), 36 (both), 37 (all), 38 (both), 39 (both), 40 (both), 41 (all), 42 (above), 43 (both); ZEFA 19 (above), 20 (both), 21 (below), 22 (below), 23 (above), 26, 42 (below), 44 (below).

The areas of water on the Earth's surface are called oceans. There are five oceans in the world. They are the Arctic, the Atlantic, the Pacific, the Indian and the Southern Oceans.

This map shows the world drawn flat on a page, but the world is really round, like a ball.

EUROPE

ASIA

Tropic of Cancer

AFRICA

Equator

INDIAN

OCEAN

Tropic of Capricorn

AUSTRALIA

SOUTHERN OCEAN

ANTARCTICA

Climate

Different parts of the world have different weather patterns called climates. Some places are hot and other places are cold, some are wet and others dry. If you lived in Greece in Europe it would be hot and dry in the summer and cooler and wetter in the winter.

Greenland is a very cold place.

KEY

Polar regions

Cold regions

Cold temperate regions

Warm temperate regions

Tropical regions

Dry regions

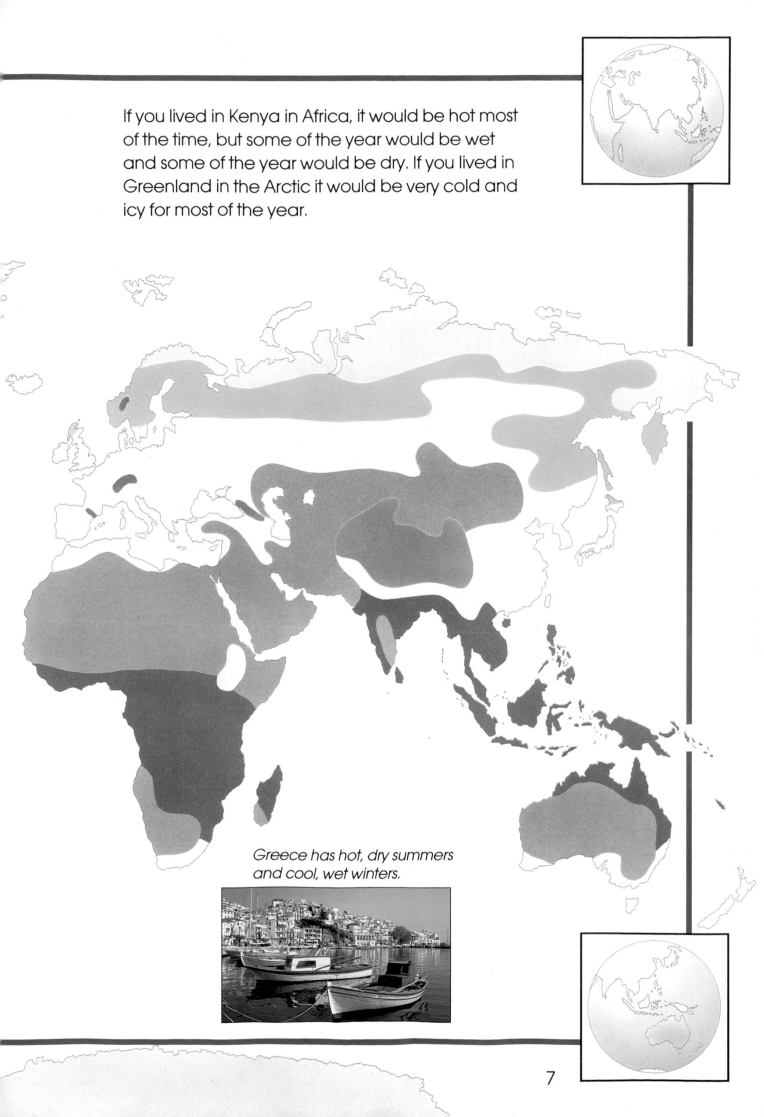

If you lived in Kenya in Africa, it would be hot most of the time, but some of the year would be wet and some of the year would be dry. If you lived in Greenland in the Arctic it would be very cold and icy for most of the year.

Greece has hot, dry summers and cool, wet winters.

7

Vegetation

Different sorts of plants grow around the world depending on whether that place is hot or cold; wet or dry. **Rainforests** are found in hot, wet areas of the world. In very cold, dry places in the world only a few plants like mosses and lichens grow.

Key

Ice and tundra

Forest

Grassland

Rainforest

Desert

The rainforest in Borneo, taken from the air.

Grassland in Kenya, Africa.

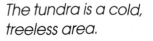

The tundra is a cold, treeless area.

Some areas have mountains and others have land that is flat. The plants that are able to grow in the mountains are different from those in the flat areas.

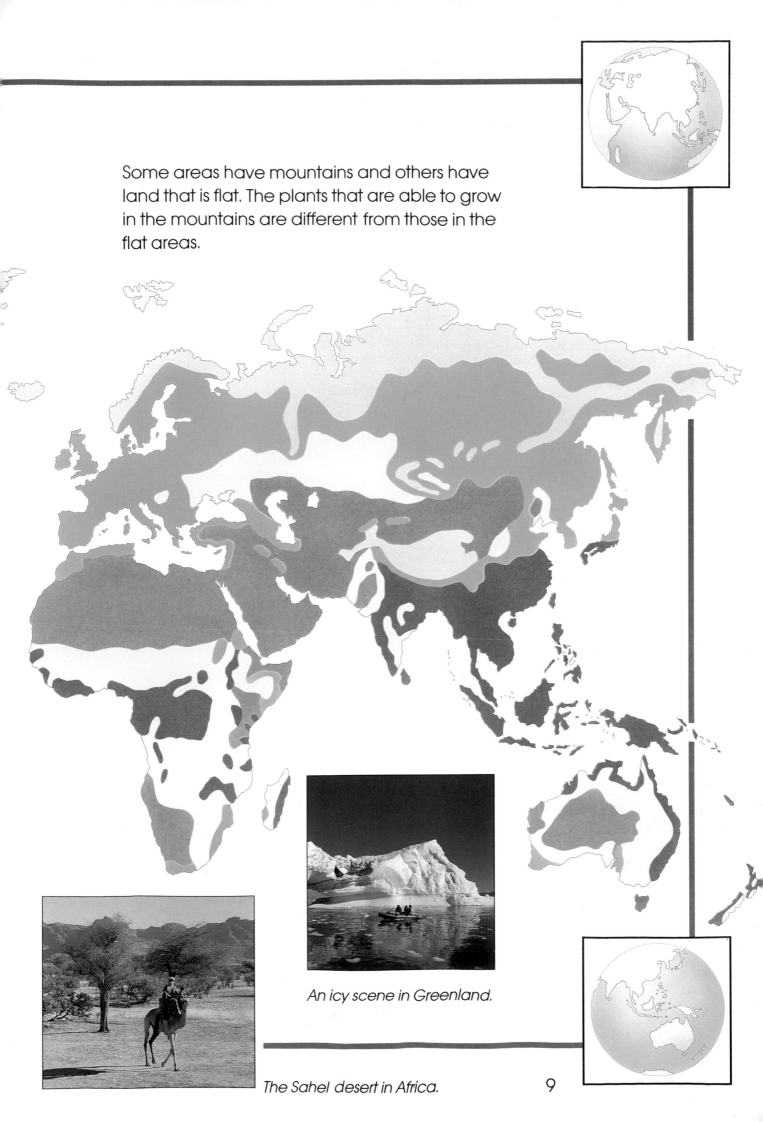

An icy scene in Greenland.

The Sahel desert in Africa.

Europe

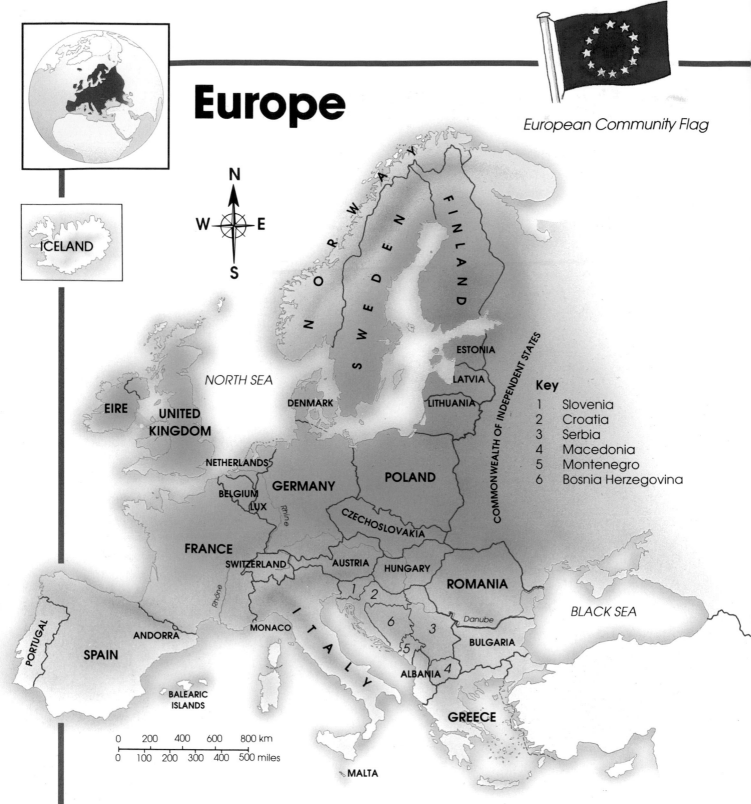

ICELAND

N
W E
S

NORTH SEA

EIRE
UNITED KINGDOM

NETHERLANDS
BELGIUM
LUX

GERMANY

FRANCE
SWITZERLAND

PORTUGAL

SPAIN

ANDORRA

MONACO

BALEARIC ISLANDS

NORWAY

SWEDEN

FINLAND

DENMARK

POLAND

CZECHOSLOVAKIA

AUSTRIA

HUNGARY

ITALY

Rhine

Rhône

ESTONIA

LATVIA

LITHUANIA

COMMONWEALTH OF INDEPENDENT STATES

Key
1 Slovenia
2 Croatia
3 Serbia
4 Macedonia
5 Montenegro
6 Bosnia Herzegovina

ROMANIA

Danube

BLACK SEA

BULGARIA

ALBANIA

GREECE

MALTA

0 200 400 600 800 km
0 100 200 300 400 500 miles

Europe is made up of many different countries. Some of these countries belong to the **European Community,** also known as the EC and sometimes called the Common Market. People from these countries meet in Brussels, Belgium, to talk about **issues** of common interest.

FACTS

Highest mt: Mt Elbrus, CIS
Longest river: Volga, CIS
Biggest city: Moscow, CIS
Country with most people: CIS
Members of the European Community: Belgium, Denmark, France, Germany, Greece, Eire, Italy, Luxembourg, the Netherlands, Portugal, Spain, UK.

The Benelux Countries

The countries of Belgium, Netherlands and Luxembourg, in northern Europe, are mainly low and flat. They are sometimes known as the Benelux countries. Much of the Netherlands is below sea level and is saved from floods by sea walls called **dykes**. Antwerp and Rotterdam are big ports where many ships bring goods in and out of Europe. There is also much industry and farming in the Benelux countries.

N
W E
S

FRISIAN ISLANDS

Groningen •

IJSSELMEER

Amsterdam •

Utrecht •

• The Hague

• Rotterdam

Waal   Lek

Maas

N E T H E R L A N D S

Eindhoven •

Cheese is an important export for the Netherlands.

Belgian chocolates are sold worldwide.

• Antwerp

• Bruges

Ostend •   • Ghent

Schelde

• Brussels

Liege •

B E L G I U M

Meuse

Windmills are a common sight in the Netherlands.

0   20   40   60   80   100km
0   10   20   30   40   50   60 miles

ARDENNES

LUXEMBOURG

Luxembourg •

FACTS

Biggest city: Brussels, Belgium
Largest country: Netherlands
Country with most people: Netherlands

The Netherlands flag

11

The British Isles

The British Isles are made up of two islands, Great Britain and Ireland. There are also a number of small islands like the Isles of Scilly and the Isle of Man. In Great Britain there are three countries; England, Wales and Scotland. Together with Northern Ireland these form the United Kingdom.

Harvesting grain crops.

FACTS

EIRE
Capital: Dublin
Highest mt: Carrauntoohil
Population: 4 million

The badger and the hedgehog are part of a rich variety of wildlife in the British Isles.

A loch in west Scotland.

The British Isles have plenty of oil in the North Sea.

FACTS

WALES
Capital: Cardiff
Highest mt: Snowdon
Population: 3 million

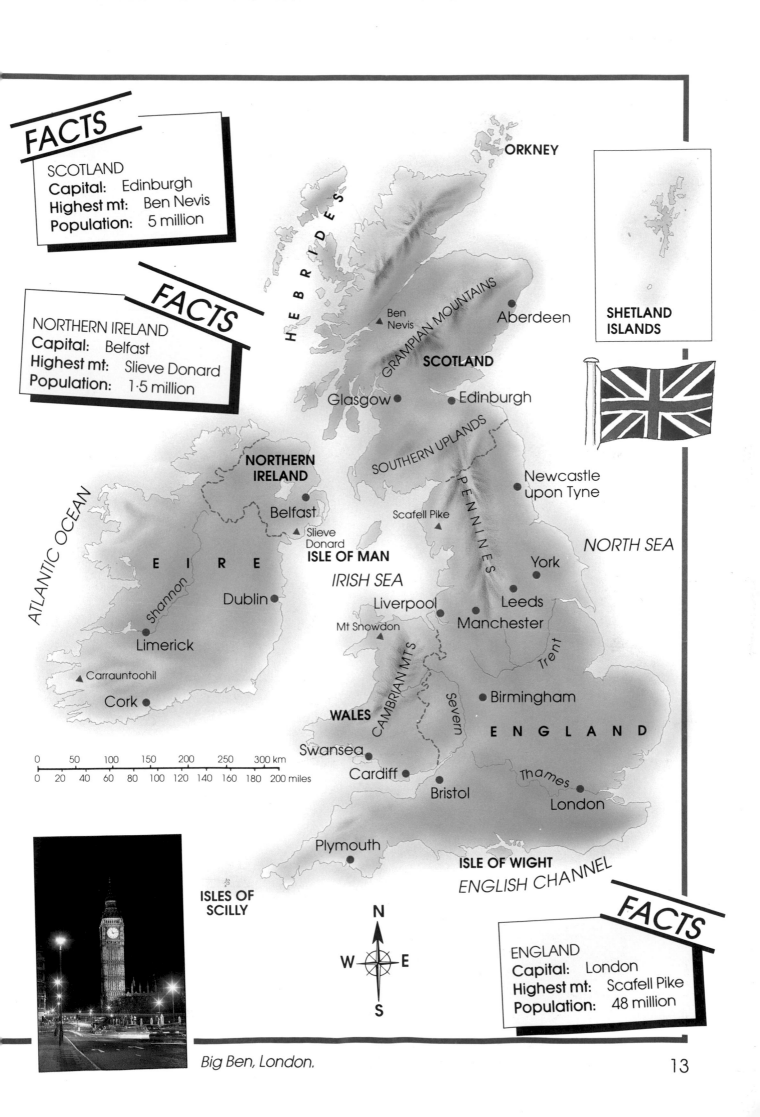

ORKNEY

SHETLAND
ISLANDS

HEBRIDES

Ben
Nevis

GRAMPIAN MOUNTAINS

Aberdeen

SCOTLAND

Glasgow

Edinburgh

SOUTHERN UPLANDS

NORTHERN
IRELAND

Belfast

Slieve
Donard

ISLE OF MAN

Scafell Pike

PENNINES

Newcastle
upon Tyne

NORTH SEA

ATLANTIC OCEAN

E I R E

Shannon

Dublin

IRISH SEA

York

Liverpool

Leeds

Limerick

Mt Snowdon

Manchester

Carrauntoohil

WALES

CAMBRIAN MTS

Trent

Birmingham

Severn

E N G L A N D

Cork

0	50	100	150	200	250	300 km
0	20 40 60 80 100 120 140 160 180					200 miles

Swansea

Cardiff

Bristol

Thames

London

Plymouth

ISLE OF WIGHT

ENGLISH CHANNEL

ISLES OF
SCILLY

N
W E
S

Big Ben, London.

France

France is the largest country in western Europe. There are three mountain ranges, called the Alps, the Pyrenees and the Massif Central, where you can walk and climb in the summer and ski in the winter. In the south of France the summers are hot and this attracts tourists from other parts of Europe. The warm climate also makes it easy to grow different crops, such as grapes. France is famous for its wines and tasty cooking.

ENGLISH CHA

CHANNEL ISLANDS

Rennes •

Nantes •

The Eiffel Tower, Paris.

N
W E
S

BAY
OF
BISCAY

Bordeaux •

Chenonceaux Chateau in the Loire Valley.

French wines are exported all over the world.

14

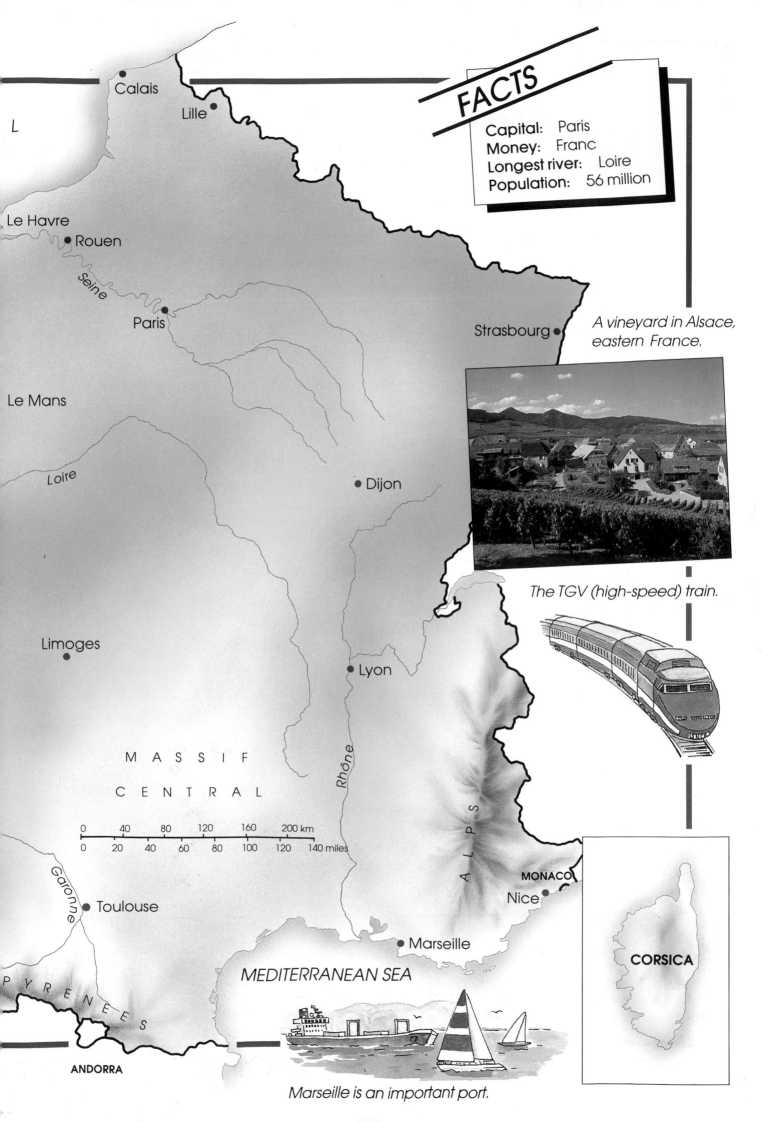

Calais

Lille

L

Le Havre

Rouen

Seine

Paris

Le Mans

Loire

Limoges

MASSIF

CENTRAL

0	40	80	120	160	200 km
0	20	40	60	80	100	120	140 miles

Garonne

Toulouse

PYRENEES

ANDORRA

Strasbourg

Dijon

Lyon

Rhône

ALPS

MONACO

Nice

Marseille

MEDITERRANEAN SEA

CORSICA

Marseille is an important port.

FACTS

Capital: Paris
Money: Franc
Longest river: Loire
Population: 56 million

A vineyard in Alsace, eastern France.

The TGV (high-speed) train.

Germany

More people live in Germany than in any other country in Europe, except for the C.I.S. There used to be two German countries, East and West Germany. In 1990 they were joined together for the first time since 1945. The country has many successful industries which make different goods, such as cars, which are sold all over the world. The big rivers of Germany have always been used for moving large and heavy goods on boats called **barges**. The River Rhine is like a motorway on water. Germany has more motorways than any other European country.

Cologne Cathedral on the River Rhine.

FACTS

Capital: Berlin
Money: Deutsch mark
Longest river: Danube
Population: 78 million

A statue in Bremen, with characters from one of Grimm's fairy tales.

The Elbe River.

Barges on the River Rhine.

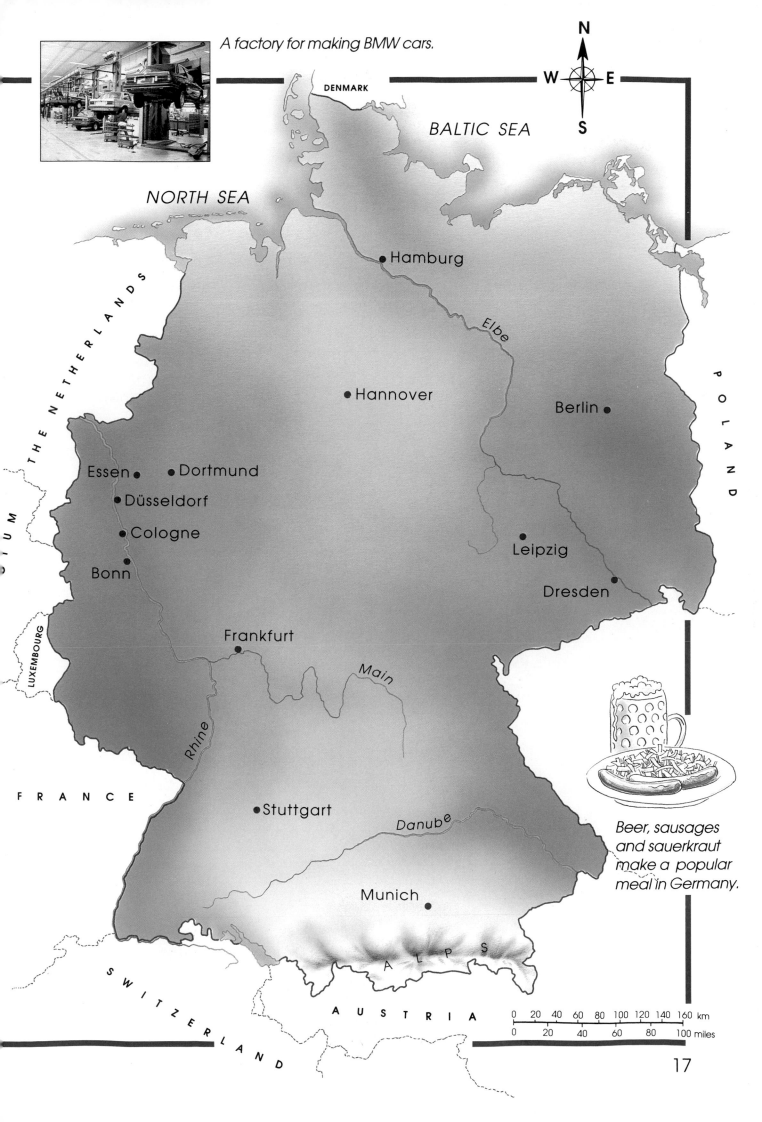

A factory for making BMW cars.

N
W   E
S

DENMARK

BALTIC SEA

NORTH SEA

THE NETHERLANDS

BELGIUM

LUXEMBOURG

FRANCE

SWITZERLAND

AUSTRIA

POLAND

• Hamburg

Elbe

• Hannover

Berlin •

Essen •   • Dortmund

• Düsseldorf

• Cologne

Bonn •

Leipzig •

Dresden •

• Frankfurt

Main

Rhine

• Stuttgart

Danube

Munich •

A L P S

Beer, sausages and sauerkraut make a popular meal in Germany.

0   20   40   60   80   100   120   140   160 km
0   20   40   60   80   100 miles

Spain and Portugal

Spain and Portugal form an area of land called the Iberian Peninsula in the south-west of Europe. There are many important industries in Spain and Portugal, such as the iron and steel works in Bilbao, and the Seat car factories. Because Spain has hot and dry summers many people from all over Europe like to go there for holidays. In 1992 the summer **Olympic Games** were held in Spain.

The Alhambra, in Granada.

Portuguese flag.

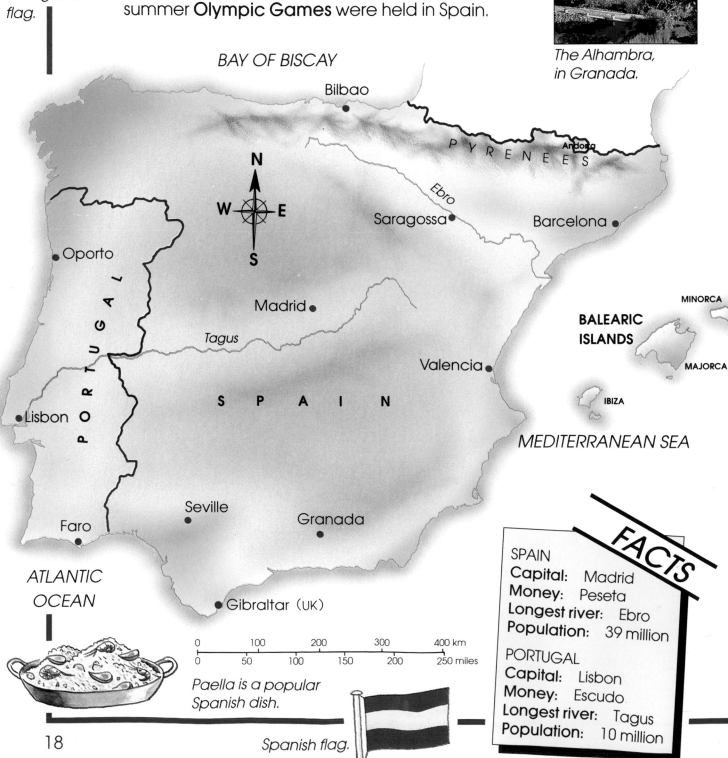

BAY OF BISCAY

Bilbao

PYRENEES

Andorra

Ebro

N

W E

S

Saragossa

Barcelona

Oporto

P O R T U G A L

Madrid

Tagus

BALEARIC ISLANDS

MINORCA

MAJORCA

Valencia

IBIZA

S P A I N

Lisbon

MEDITERRANEAN SEA

Seville

Granada

Faro

ATLANTIC OCEAN

Gibraltar (UK)

0	100	200	300	400 km
0	50	100	150	200	250 miles

Paella is a popular Spanish dish.

FACTS

SPAIN
Capital: Madrid
Money: Peseta
Longest river: Ebro
Population: 39 million

PORTUGAL
Capital: Lisbon
Money: Escudo
Longest river: Tagus
Population: 10 million

Spanish flag.

Italy

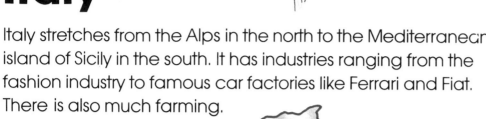

Italy stretches from the Alps in the north to the Mediterranean island of Sicily in the south. It has industries ranging from the fashion industry to famous car factories like Ferrari and Fiat. There is also much farming.

St. Mark's Square, Venice.

Italy is famous for its many types of pasta.

DOLOMITES

ALPS

Lake Garda

Milan

Turin

Verona

Venice

Po

N

W E

S

Genoa

A
P
E
N
N
I
N
E
S

ADRIATIC SEA

MONACO

SAN MARINO

Florence

Arno

SARDINIA

I
T
A
L
Y

Tiber

Rome

MEDITERRANEAN SEA

Bari

Naples ▲ Mt Vesuvius

Taranto

Italy has many historic remains, such as the Colosseum in Rome.

FACTS

Capital:	Rome
Money:	Lira
Longest river:	Po
Population:	57 million

Palermo

Mt Etna ▲

SICILY

0	100	200	300 km
0	50	100	150	200 miles

19

Scandinavia and the Baltic States

There are five countries which make up Scandinavia – Iceland, Finland, Norway, Sweden and Denmark. These countries are very cold in the winter and have a lot of snow and ice in the forests and mountains. Much of the land is covered with forests, mountains and lakes. There are sea inlets called **fiords** in Norway. There is good farmland in the south of Sweden which is used for growing wheat and sugar beet. Dairy farming is important in Denmark and Sweden. Scandinavia has many important natural **resources** such as fish, **iron ore** in Sweden and oil and gas fields in the North Sea.

A hot spring erupting in Iceland.

A city scene in the capital of Sweden, Stockholm.

FACTS

Highest mt: Glittertind, Norway
Biggest city: Stockholm, Sweden
Largest country: Sweden
Country with most people: Sweden

There are still some people in the far north of Sweden, Norway and Finland who are reindeer farmers. They are called Lapps.

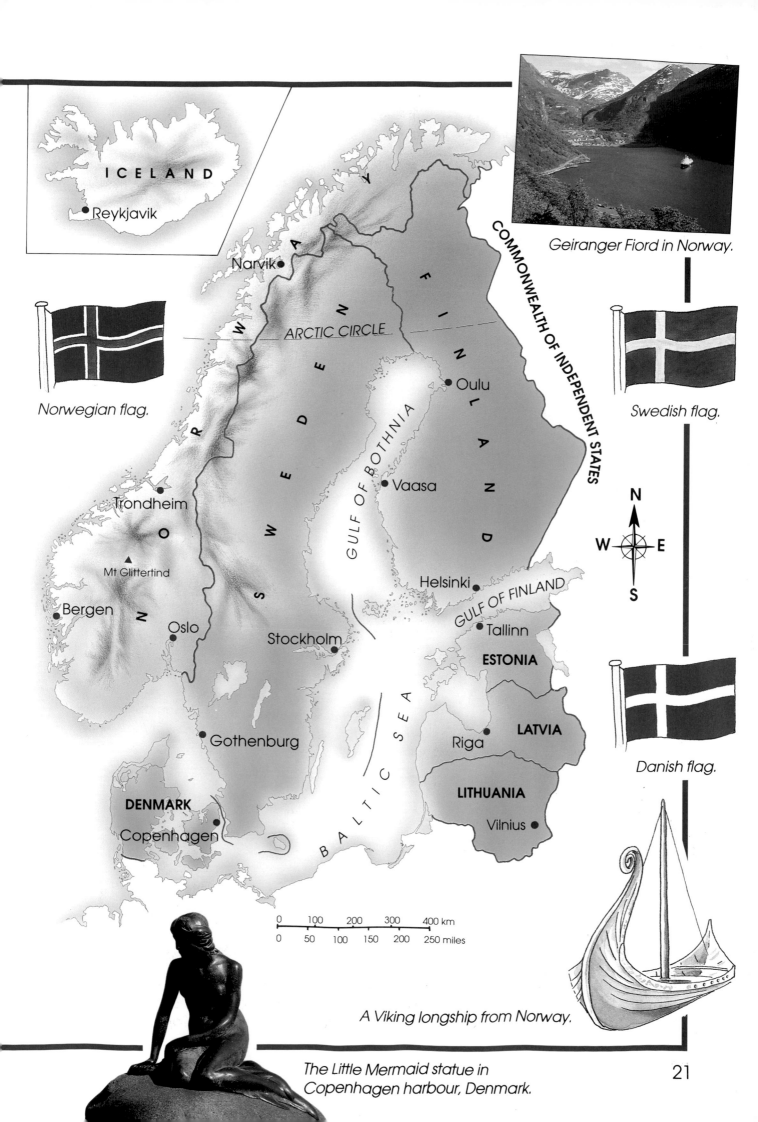

ICELAND

Reykjavik

Geiranger Fiord in Norway.

Norwegian flag.

Swedish flag.

COMMONWEALTH OF INDEPENDENT STATES

ARCTIC CIRCLE

Narvik

N O R W A Y

S W E D E N

F I N L A N D

Oulu

GULF OF BOTHNIA

Vaasa

Trondheim

Mt Glittertind

Bergen

Oslo

Helsinki

GULF OF FINLAND

Tallinn

ESTONIA

N

W — E

S

Stockholm

Gothenburg

Riga

LATVIA

Danish flag.

B A L T I C   S E A

LITHUANIA

DENMARK

Copenhagen

Vilnius

| 0 | 100 | 200 | 300 | 400 km |
| 0 | 50 | 100 | 150 | 200 | 250 miles |

A Viking longship from Norway.

The Little Mermaid statue in Copenhagen harbour, Denmark.

Central and Eastern Europe

The longest river in central and eastern Europe flows right through this area. It is called the Danube. There are many historic towns and cities in this part of Europe: Warsaw in Poland, Budapest in Hungary and Athens in Greece. Poland has many valuable resources such as copper and coal, and has shipbuilding, steel and iron industries. Poland and Hungary have big areas of flat land which are good for farming. In Greece many farmers grow grapes for making wine. Greece also has a large tourist industry.

The main square in Prague, the capital of Czechoslovakia.

FACTS

Longest river: Danube
Biggest city: Budapest, Hungary
Largest country: Poland
Country with most people:
   Poland

A wild boar in a Romanian forest.

The Hungarian capital Budapest on the River Danube.

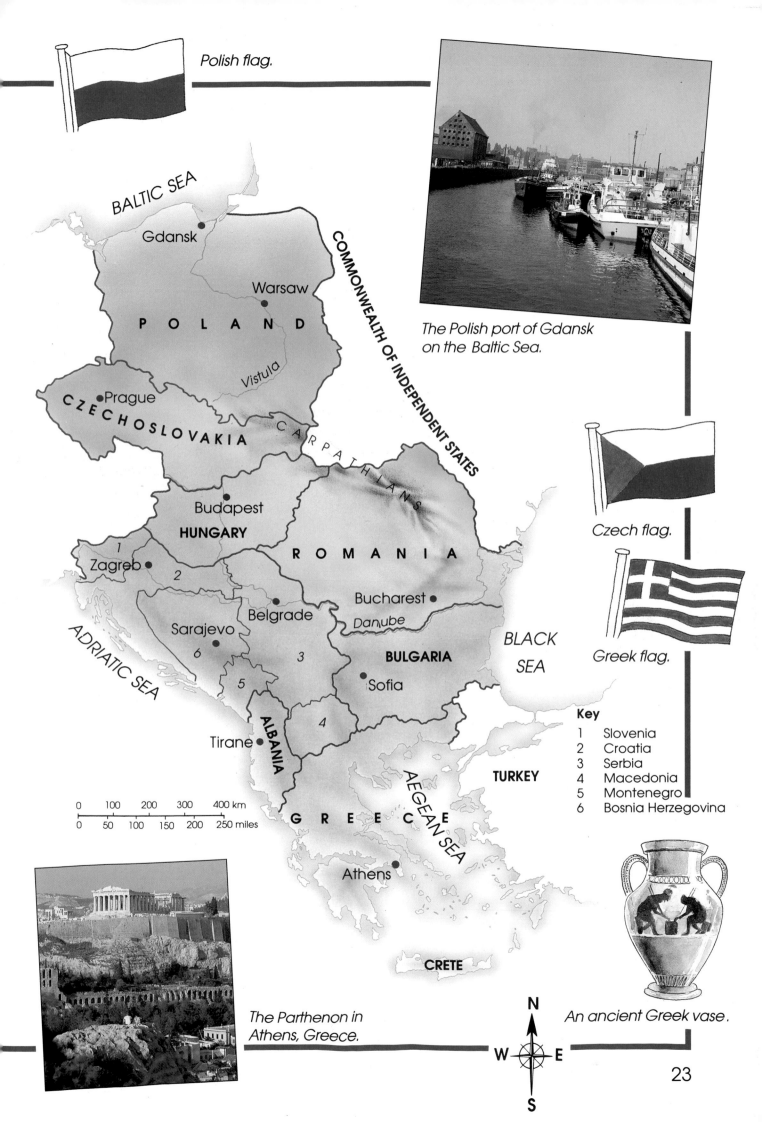

Polish flag.

BALTIC SEA

Gdansk

The Polish port of Gdansk on the Baltic Sea.

Warsaw

P O L A N D

Vistula

COMMONWEALTH OF INDEPENDENT STATES

CZECHOSLOVAKIA

Prague

CARPATHIANS

Budapest

HUNGARY

Czech flag.

R O M A N I A

1

Zagreb

2

Bucharest

Belgrade

Danube

Greek flag.

Sarajevo

6

3

BULGARIA

BLACK SEA

5

Sofia

4

ALBANIA

Tirane

Key

1   Slovenia
2   Croatia
3   Serbia
4   Macedonia
5   Montenegro
6   Bosnia Herzegovina

TURKEY

ADRIATIC SEA

AEGEAN SEA

| 0 | 100 | 200 | 300 | 400 km |
| 0 | 50 | 100 | 150 | 200 | 250 miles |

G R E E C E

Athens

CRETE

The Parthenon in Athens, Greece.

An ancient Greek vase.

W   E
N
S

Canada

Canada is the world's second largest country, but it does not have a large population. Most people live in the east of Canada by the Great Lakes and St. Lawrence River. Large areas in the north of Canada are very cold and few people live there.

FACTS

Capital: Ottawa
Money: Canadian dollar
Highest mt: Mt Logan
Largest city: Toronto
Population: 26 million

A caribou.

A timber mill on the west coast near Vancouver.

ALASKA (USA)

YUKON TERRITORY

▲ Mt Logan

NORTHWEST

Yellowknife

ROCKY MOUNTAINS

BRITISH COLUMBIA

ALBERTA

Edmonton

SASKATCHEWAN

Calgary

Vancouver

C A N

U S A

N
W E
S

A grizzly bear.

The high Rocky Mountains are found in the west. In the centre of Canada there is flat land called the **prairies** which is used for farming. After farming, mining is the most important industry. Forestry and fishing are important too.

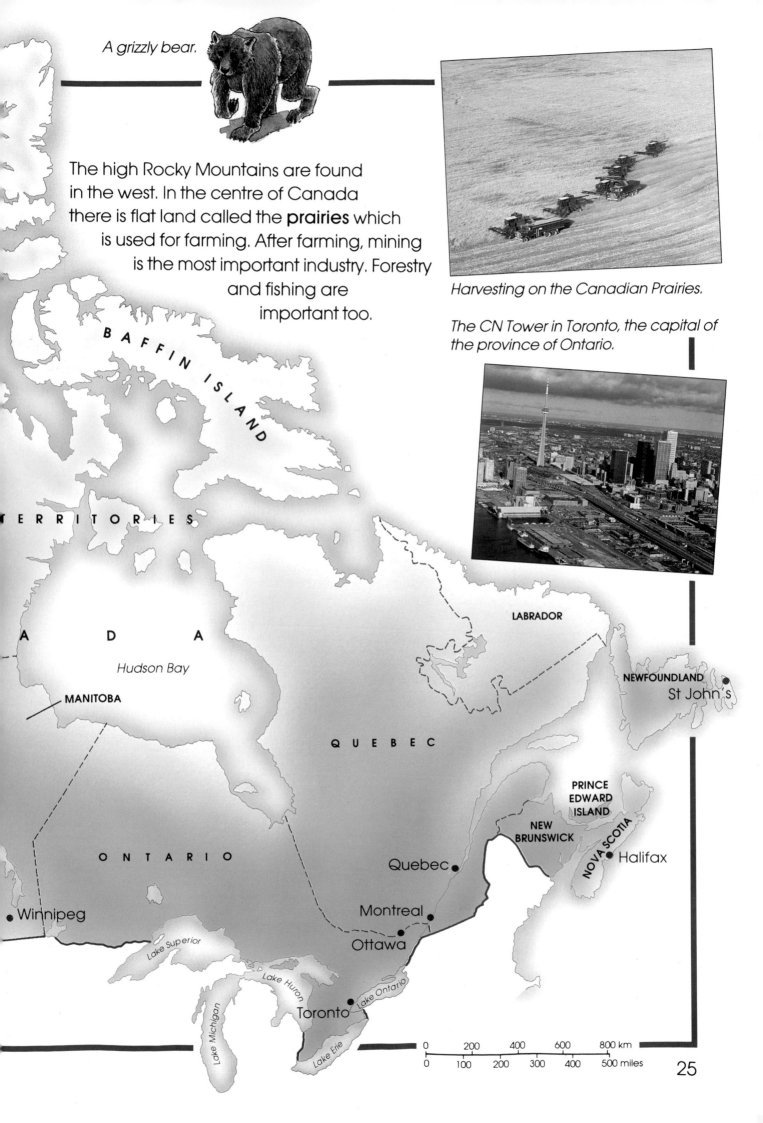

Harvesting on the Canadian Prairies.

The CN Tower in Toronto, the capital of the province of Ontario.

BAFFIN ISLAND

ERRITORIES

A   D   A

Hudson Bay

MANITOBA

LABRADOR

NEWFOUNDLAND
St John's

QUEBEC

PRINCE EDWARD ISLAND

NEW BRUNSWICK

NOVA SCOTIA

Halifax

ONTARIO

Quebec

Montreal

Winnipeg

Lake Superior

Ottawa

Lake Huron

Lake Michigan

Lake Ontario

Toronto

Lake Erie

0	200	400	600	800 km
0	100	200	300	400	500 miles

The United States of America

People from many parts of the world have joined the original people of the U.S.A. It is made up of fifty different states, including Alaska and Hawaii.

In many big cities, such as New York and Chicago, the buildings are so tall they seem to touch the sky. They are called skyscrapers. Land in the cities is very expensive, so it is cheaper to build upwards rather than outwards.

As the USA is such a huge country it has many different climates and many types of farming. For example cotton comes from Texas, Arizona, New Mexico and California. Wheat and maize are grown on the prairies, which are found in the north of the USA between the Rocky Mountains and the Great Lakes.

The bald eagle is the symbol of the U.S.A.

ALASKA

Anchorage

0 200 400 600 800km
0   200   400miles

MONTANA

WASHINGTON

OREGON

R O C K Y

IDAHO

SIERRA NEVADA

CALIFORNIA

NEVADA

UTAH

M O U N T A I N S

Colorado

San Francisco

Los Angeles

ARIZONA

Phoenix

NEW MEXIC

PACIFIC OCEAN

Honolulu

HAWAII

0   80   160   240   320km
0   50   100   150   200miles

The Grand Canyon in Arizona.

FACTS

Capital: Washington DC
Money: US dollar
Longest river: Mississippi
Largest state: Alaska
Population: 246 million

Hamburger and cola.

The New York skyline.

0 200 400 600 800 1000 km
0 100 200 300 400 500 600 miles

N.H. = NEW HAMPSHIRE
MASS. = MASSACHUSETTS
R.I. = RHODE ISLAND
CONN. = CONNECTICUT
DEL. = DELAWARE

The Statue of Liberty, New York.

NORTH DAKOTA
MINNESOTA
Lake Superior
MICHIGAN
Lake Michigan
Lake Huron
MAINE

SOUTH DAKOTA
WISCONSIN
VERMONT
N.H.

WYO-MING
IOWA
Lake Ontario
NEW YORK
MASS.
R.I.
CONN.

NEBRASKA
Chicago
Lake Erie
PENNSYLVANIA
New York
NEW JERSEY

COLORADO
Missouri
ILLINOIS
INDIANA
OHIO
Washington DC
MARYLAND
DEL.

KANSAS
MISSOURI
WEST VIRGINIA
VIRGINIA

OKLAHOMA
ARKANSAS
KENTUCKY
APPALACHIAN MTS
NORTH CAROLINA

Mississippi
TENNESSEE
SOUTH CAROLINA

Dallas
ALABAMA
GEORGIA
ATLANTIC OCEAN

TEXAS
MISSISSIPPI
LOUISIANA

Rio Grande
Houston

MEXICO

GULF OF MEXICO
FLORIDA
Miami

A paddle steamer on the Mississippi.

The Space Shuttle.

27

Central America and the Caribbean

The countries of Central America lie on a narrow strip of land between the two continents of North and South America. At the narrowest point the Panama Canal has been built to join the Pacific and Atlantic Oceans.

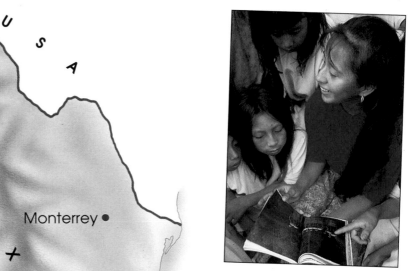

Mayan children at school in southern Mexico.

USA

MEXICO

Monterrey ●

●Guadalajara

Mexico City
●
Popocatepetl ◢

● Acapulco

GULF OF MEXICO

BELIZE

GUATEMALA

HONDURAS

San Salvador ●
EL SALVADOR

Managua ●

PACIFIC OCEAN

N
W ✦ E
S

Working on an oil rig in Mexico.

An ancient Mexican temple.

28

A Mexican chilli shop selling over thirty different varieties.

An armadillo.

Mexican flag.

Mexico City is the world's largest city. Much oil is found in Mexico and there are many factories around Mexico City. Many historic remains have been found of people like the **Mayas** who lived in this area a long time ago. The Caribbean islands are found off the east coast of Central America. Many people in the Caribbean islands are farmers. They grow crops which need a lot of sun, such as sugar-cane and coconuts.

A fruit stall in a Jamaican market.

The Caribbean islands have beautiful beaches.

FACTS

Largest volcano: Popocatepetl, Mexico
Biggest city: Mexico City, Mexico
Largest island: Cuba
Country with most people: Mexico

THE BAHAMAS
Nassau

C U B A

ATLANTIC OCEAN

PUERTO RICO

HAITI   DOMINICAN REPUBLIC

ANTIGUA

GUADELOUPE

DOMINICA

JAMAICA
Kingston

MARTINIQUE

ST LUCIA

ST VINCENT & THE GRENADINES   BARBADOS

GRENADA

```
0      200      400      600      800 km
0    100   200   300   400   500 miles
```

C A R I B B E A N   S E A

TRINIDAD & TOBAGO

NICARAGUA

COSTA RICA

SOUTH AMERICA

Panama Canal   Panama City

PANAMA

A ship passing through the Panama Canal.

29

South America

The continent of South America is made up of thirteen countries. There are very high mountains, deserts and hot, wet forests in this area. South America's large cities are found mainly on, or near, the coast. Although most people live in cities, many South Americans are farmers. Some work on large farms called **plantations** but most farms are very small plots of land where people grow their own food.

The area is rich in historic sites, such as the famous **Inca** remains in Peru.

Llamas in the high mountains of the Andes.

A coffee farm and freshly-picked coffee. Brazil produces the most coffee in the world.

◄ *The Amazon rainforest, Brazil.*

A macaw.

FACTS

Highest mt: Aconcagua, Argentina
Longest river: Amazon
Largest forest: Amazon
Biggest city: São Paulo, Brazil
Largest country: Brazil
Country with most people: Brazil

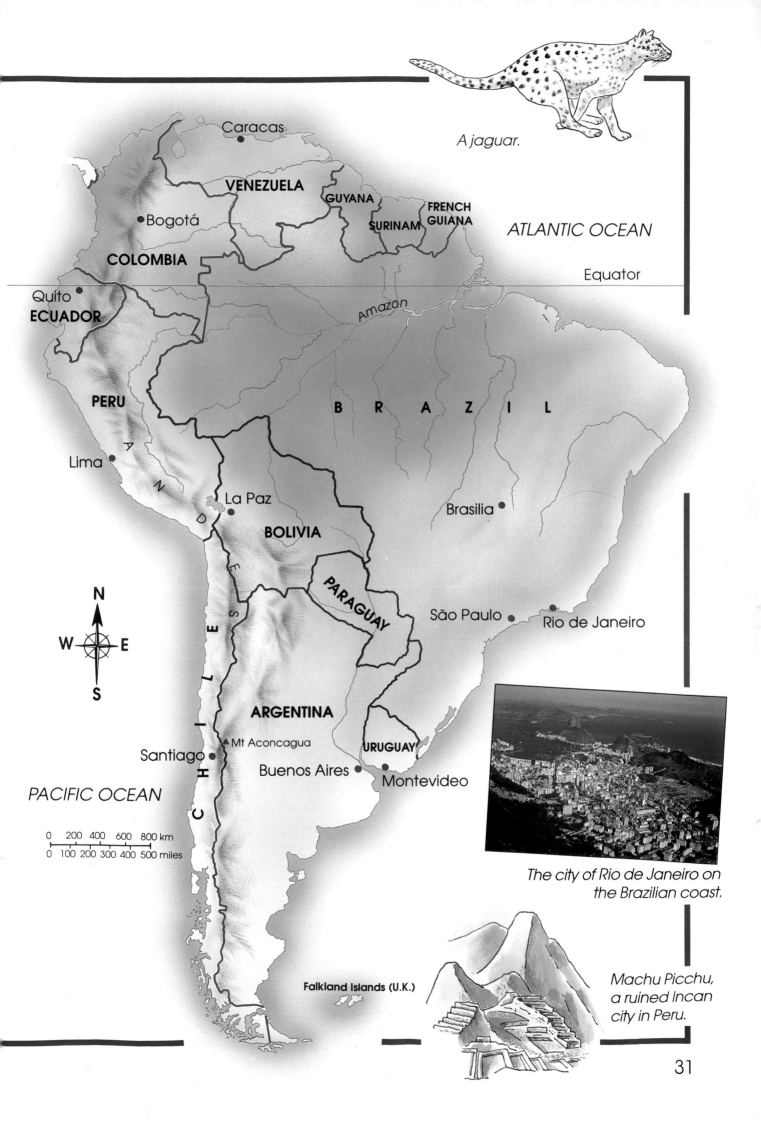

A jaguar.

Caracas

VENEZUELA

GUYANA

SURINAM

FRENCH
GUIANA

ATLANTIC OCEAN

Equator

Bogotá

COLOMBIA

Quito

ECUADOR

Amazon

PERU

B R A Z I L

Lima

A
N
D
E
S

La Paz

BOLIVIA

Brasilia

PARAGUAY

São Paulo

Rio de Janeiro

N

W   E

S

C
H
I
L
E

ARGENTINA

Mt Aconcagua

URUGUAY

Santiago

Buenos Aires

Montevideo

PACIFIC OCEAN

0   200 400   600 800 km
0   100 200 300 400 500 miles

Falkland Islands (U.K.)

The city of Rio de Janeiro on
the Brazilian coast.

Machu Picchu,
a ruined Incan
city in Peru.

Africa

This huge continent is made up of many different countries. It has very large deserts such as the Sahara and the Kalahari, and huge areas of hot, wet rainforests near the **Equator**. There are many important resources in African countries, such as oil in Nigeria and Libya, copper in Zaire and Zambia and iron ore in Mauritania. There are some very large cities in Africa such as Cairo, Lagos, Nairobi and Johannesburg. Many Africans are also farmers and live in small communities. The continent has a rich variety of animals and birds.

Tourism is a valuable industry for Kenya.

FACTS

Highest mt: Kilimanjaro, Tanzania
Longest river: Nile
Biggest city: Cairo, Egypt
Largest country: Sudan
Largest desert: Sahara
Country with most people: Nigeria

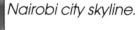

Nairobi city skyline.

A mountain gorilla in Rwanda.

A zebra.

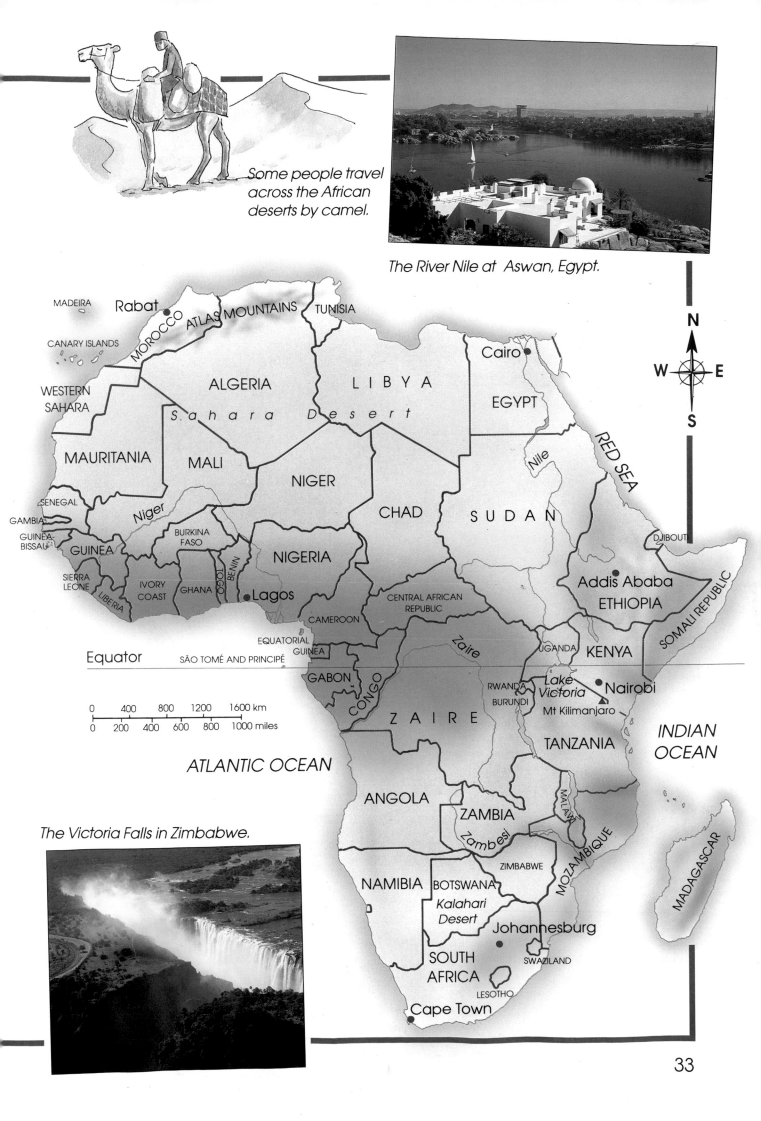

Some people travel across the African deserts by camel.

The River Nile at Aswan, Egypt.

MADEIRA

Rabat
MOROCCO   ATLAS MOUNTAINS   TUNISIA

CANARY ISLANDS

Cairo

WESTERN
SAHARA

ALGERIA   L I B Y A

EGYPT

S a h a r a   D e s e r t

MAURITANIA   MALI

NIGER

Nile

RED SEA

SENEGAL

Niger

CHAD

S U D A N

GAMBIA

GUINEA-
BISSAU

GUINEA

BURKINA
FASO

NIGERIA

DJIBOUTI

SIERRA
LEONE

IVORY
COAST

GHANA
TOGO
BENIN

Lagos

CENTRAL AFRICAN
REPUBLIC

Addis Ababa

ETHIOPIA

LIBERIA

CAMEROON

SOMALI REPUBLIC

Equator   SÃO TOMÉ AND PRINCIPÉ

EQUATORIAL
GUINEA

Zaire

UGANDA   KENYA

GABON

CONGO

RWANDA
BURUNDI

Lake
Victoria

Nairobi

Mt Kilimanjaro

0   400   800   1200   1600 km

0   200   400   600   800   1000 miles

Z A I R E

TANZANIA

INDIAN
OCEAN

ATLANTIC OCEAN

ANGOLA

ZAMBIA

MALAWI

The Victoria Falls in Zimbabwe.

Zambesi

MOZAMBIQUE

ZIMBABWE

MADAGASCAR

NAMIBIA   BOTSWANA

*Kalahari
Desert*

Johannesburg

SWAZILAND

SOUTH
AFRICA

LESOTHO

Cape Town

N
W   E
S

33

Commonwealth of Independent States

Several **independent** states, once known as the Soviet Union, now form the Commonwealth of Independent States. They cover one-seventh of the world's land area. The largest state is Russia with 145 million people. It stretches from Finland to Alaska and from the Arctic Ocean to China. Russia has immense oil and gas fields, much good farmland and many important **raw materials.**

Wild wolves can still be found in the CIS.

The Cathedral of the Annunciation, Moscow.

Arkhangelsk

St. Petersburg

Moscow

Minsk

Kiev

Kishinev

BLACK SEA

Tbilisi

Yerevan

Baku

Ashkhabad

CASPIAN SEA

ARAL SEA

Tashkent

LAKE BALKHASH

Alma-Ata

Frunze

Dushanbe

Communism Peak

Omsk

URAL MTS.

Volga

Don

Irtysh

Ob

5

2

4

7

6

11

3

10

8

A snow leopard.

The desert in winter, Kazakhstan.

The second largest state is the Ukraine centred around Kiev. On the borders of Afghanistan and China are the six **Muslim** states, the largest of which is Kazakhstan.

Walruses live near the Arctic Ocean.

ARCTIC OCEAN

SIBERIAN UPLANDS

Key to CIS States

1	Russia
2	Ukraine
3	Uzbekistan
4	Kazakhstan
5	Belorussia
6	Azerbaijan
7	Georgia
8	Tadzhikstan
9	Moldova
10	Kirgizstan
11	Turkmenistan
12	Armenia

Lena

Yenisey

LAKE BAIKAL

Amur

ALTAI MTS

Yakutsk

0	400	800	1200	1600	2000	2400 km
0	250	500	750	1000	1250	1500 miles

BERING SEA

SEA OF OKHOTSK

Vladivostok

FACTS

Largest city: Moscow, Russia
Largest lake: Caspian Sea
(the largest lake in the world)
Longest river: Yenisey
Highest mountain: Communism Peak, Tadzhikstan

Matrioshka dolls.

35

Indian flag.

Southern Asia

Nearly one-quarter of the world's people live in this region. The largest country in Southern Asia is India and the smallest is Bhutan. The Himalayas is the highest mountain range in the world. Two long rivers flow from these mountains into large flat plains which are ideal for farming. Most people in Southern Asia depend on farming and the most important crop is rice. Rice needs a lot of water and this comes from the **monsoon** rains. Pakistan and India are the most industrial countries in this area and both have important textile industries. India also produces coal, iron ore and copper.

FACTS

Highest mt: Everest, in Nepal and China
Longest river: Indus, Pakistan
Biggest city: Calcutta, India
Largest country: India
Country with most people: India

Worshipping at a mosque in Pakistan.

A material shop in India.

The Taj Mahal, in Northern India, was built as a tomb for an emperor's wife. It took twenty years to build and was finished in 1650.

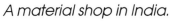

The Golden Temple, Amritsar, India.

A tiger.

A mountain valley in the Himalayas.

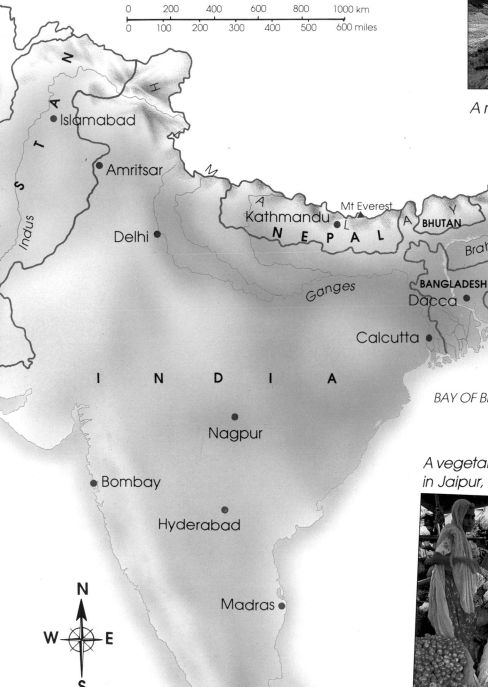

```
0      200    400    600    800    1000 km
0    100   200   300   400   500   600 miles
```

PAKISTAN

• Islamabad

H

• Amritsar

Indus

Delhi •

Kathmandu
Mt Everest

A L A Y A S

NEPAL

BHUTAN

Brahmaputra

Ganges

BANGLADESH

Dacca •

Mandalay •

Calcutta •

MYANMAR
(Burma)

I N D I A

BAY OF BENGAL

Nagpur •

Rangoon •

A vegetable market in Jaipur, India.

Bombay •

Hyderabad •

N

W — E

S

Madras •

SRI LANKA

Colombo •

South-West Asia

South-West Asia is the meeting place of the three continents, Africa, Asia and Europe, and is sometimes known as the Middle East. It was in this area that farming first took place along the Rivers Tigris and Euphrates. There are large deserts in this area which have extremely high temperatures. The region is rich in oil, which is sold all over the world. South-West Asia is the home of the Muslim religion, with Mecca in Saudi Arabia as its most holy place. Jerusalem is also a holy city for Christians, Jews and **Muslims**.

FACTS

Biggest city:
Tehran, Iran
Largest country:
Saudi Arabia

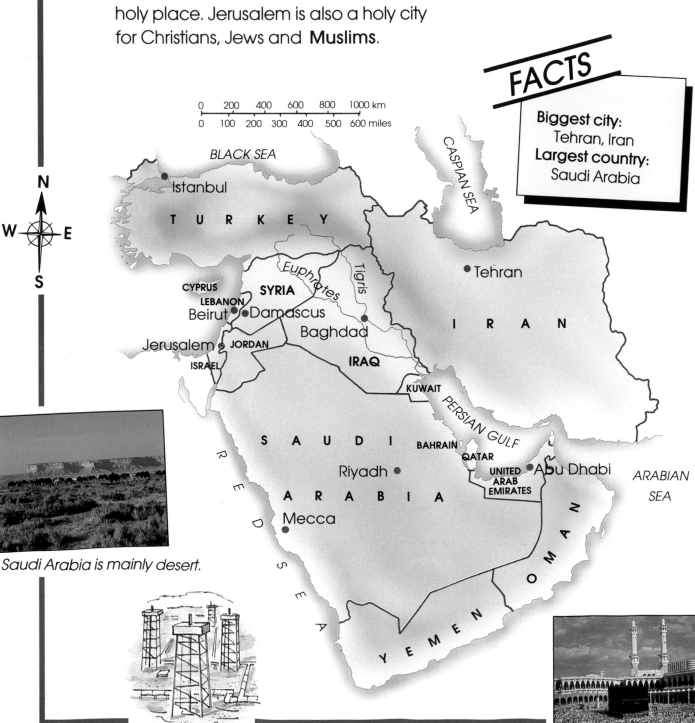

Saudi Arabia is mainly desert.

Oil wells in Saudi Arabia.

Muslims worshipping at Mecca.

South-East Asia

There are thousands of islands in this area, from the large island of New Guinea to the many smaller islands which make up the Philippines. The region lies on the Equator and is hot and wet for all of the year. Much of the land is covered in forests. There are some very important ports like Singapore and large cities like Jakarta in Indonesia. Many people earn their living from fishing or farming.

FACTS

Longest river: Mekong
Biggest city: Jakarta, Indonesia
Largest country: Indonesia
Country with most people:
    Indonesia

LAOS

VIETNAM

SOUTH CHINA SEA

THAILAND
Bangkok

Mekong

CAMBODIA

Ho Chi-minh City

Manila

PHILIPPINES

MALAYSIA

MALAYA

Kuala Lumpur

BRUNEI

SARAWAK

SINGAPORE

BORNEO

INDONESIA

Jakarta

JAVA

NEW | GUINEA
PAPUA
NEW GUINEA

Equator

A leatherback turtle.

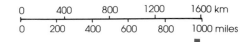

| 0 | 400 | 800 | 1200 | 1600 km |
| 0 | 200 | 400 | 600 | 800 | 1000 miles |

A Hindu temple in Indonesia.

Growing rice in Bali.

N
W E
S

39

The Far East

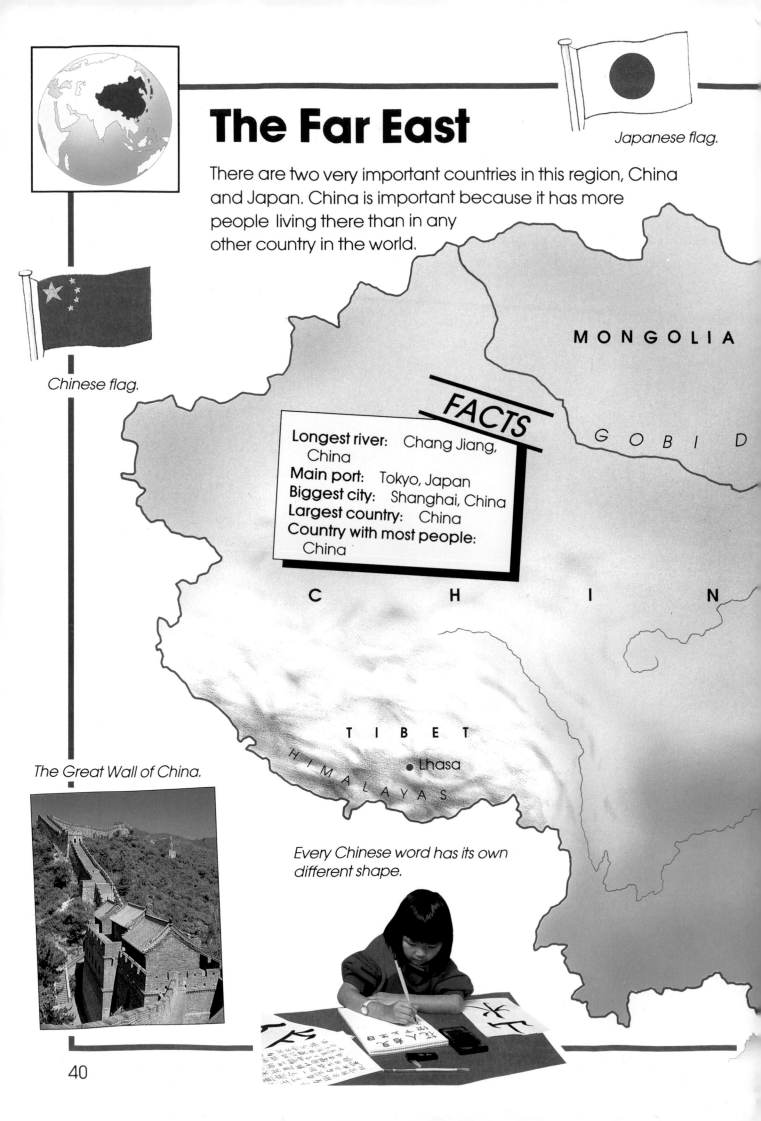

Japanese flag.

There are two very important countries in this region, China and Japan. China is important because it has more people living there than in any other country in the world.

Chinese flag.

MONGOLIA

GOBI D

FACTS

Longest river: Chang Jiang, China
Main port: Tokyo, Japan
Biggest city: Shanghai, China
Largest country: China
Country with most people: China

C   H   I   N

T I B E T

HIMALAYAS

• Lhasa

The Great Wall of China.

Every Chinese word has its own different shape.

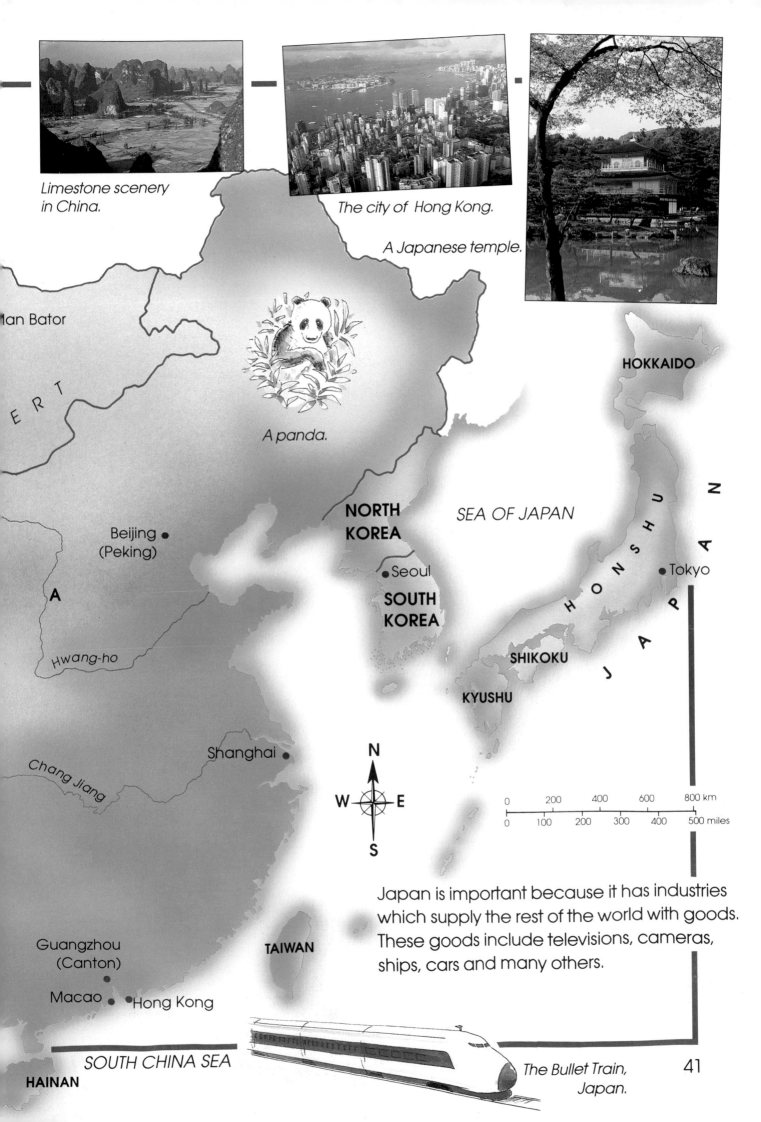

Limestone scenery
in China.

The city of Hong Kong.

A Japanese temple.

lan Bator

HOKKAIDO

A panda.

NORTH
KOREA

SEA OF JAPAN

Beijing
(Peking)

Seoul

SOUTH
KOREA

Tokyo

A

H
O
N
S
H
U

J
A
P
A
N

Hwang-ho

SHIKOKU

KYUSHU

Shanghai

N

W   E

S

0   200   400   600   800 km

0   100   200   300   400   500 miles

Chang Jiang

Japan is important because it has industries
which supply the rest of the world with goods.
These goods include televisions, cameras,
ships, cars and many others.

Guangzhou
(Canton)

TAIWAN

Macao
Hong Kong

SOUTH CHINA SEA

HAINAN

The Bullet Train,
Japan.

41

Australia and New Zealand

Australian flag.

Australia is the world's smallest continent. It has very few people living in it in relation to its size. The largest number of people live in cities in the south-east of Australia, such as Sydney and Melbourne. There are large deserts covering much of the continent. New Zealand is made up of two islands and most of the people live in the North Island, in the cities of Auckland and Wellington. The first people to live in Australia were Aborigines. In New Zealand the first people were the Maori.

Darwin

Great Sandy Desert

WESTERN | Alice Springs

Gibson Desert   Ayers Rock ▲

A U S T

Great Victoria Desert

A U S T R A L I A

● Perth

SOUTH AUSTRALIA

Mining iron ore in west Australia.

The city of Brisbane.

FACTS

Highest mt: Mt Cook, New Zealand
Longest river: Murray Darling, Australia
Biggest city: Sydney, Australia
Largest country: Australia
Country with most people: Australia

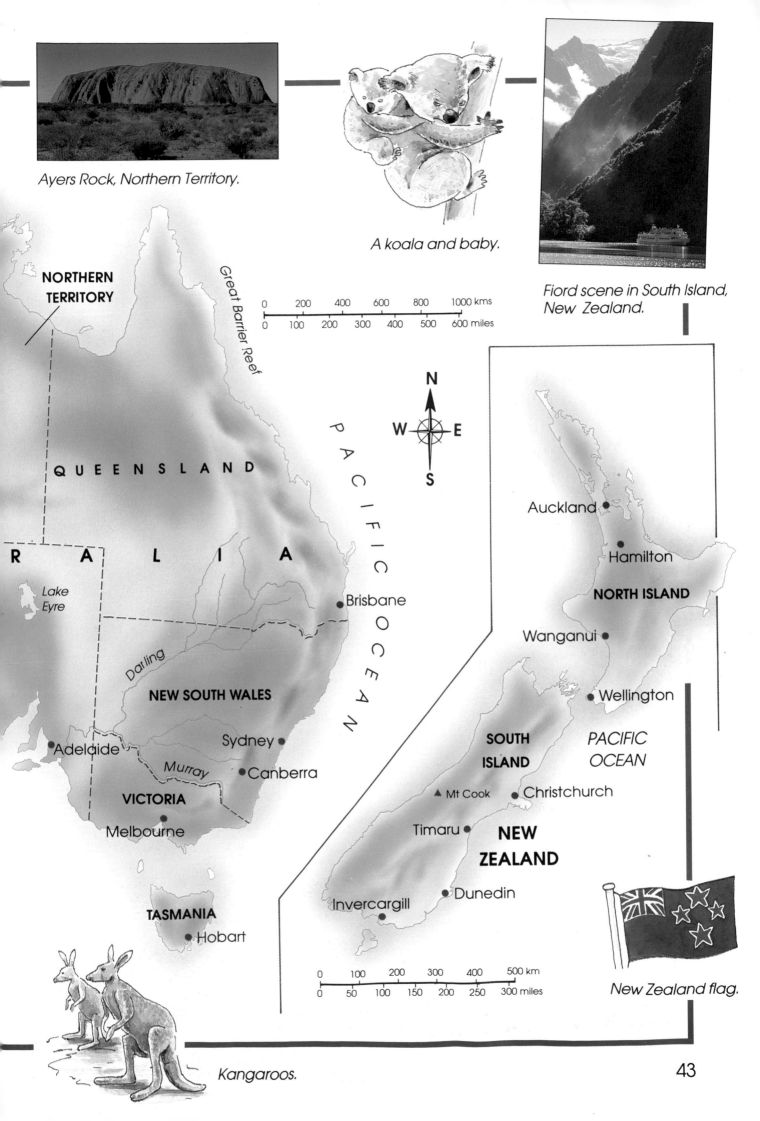

Ayers Rock, Northern Territory.

A koala and baby.

Fiord scene in South Island, New Zealand.

NORTHERN TERRITORY

Great Barrier Reef

0   200   400   600   800   1000 kms
0   100   200   300   400   500   600 miles

QUEENSLAND

R A L I A

Lake Eyre

Brisbane

Darling

NEW SOUTH WALES

Adelaide

Murray

Sydney

Canberra

VICTORIA

Melbourne

TASMANIA

Hobart

N
W   E
S

PACIFIC OCEAN

Auckland

Hamilton

NORTH ISLAND

Wanganui

Wellington

SOUTH ISLAND

PACIFIC OCEAN

▲ Mt Cook

Christchurch

Timaru

NEW ZEALAND

Invercargill

Dunedin

0   100   200   300   400   500 km
0   50   100   150   200   250   300 miles

New Zealand flag.

Kangaroos.

43

The Arctic

A polar bear.

At the northern tip of the globe is the Arctic. Most of this region is water, but as the temperatures are so low it is usually covered in ice. There is no land at the North Pole. Most people living in this area are hunters like the **Inuit** people.
There is little farming.

Inuit children playing on the ice.

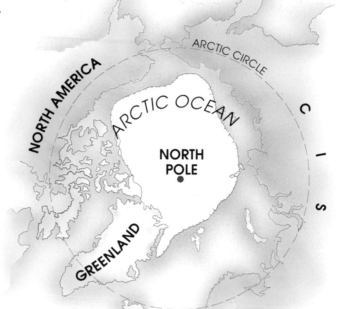

NORTH AMERICA

ARCTIC CIRCLE

ARCTIC OCEAN

NORTH POLE

GREENLAND

The Antarctic

The Antarctic is the coldest region in the world. Most of the ice in the world is found on top of the land surface of Antarctica. In places the ice can be 2.5 km thick. Scientists are the only people living in the Antarctic. No one stays longer than a few years as it is a very cold and lonely place to work.

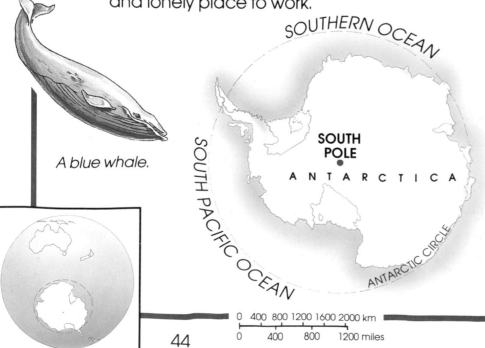

SOUTHERN OCEAN

SOUTH PACIFIC OCEAN

SOUTH POLE

ANTARCTICA

ANTARCTIC CIRCLE

A blue whale.

A scientist and an emperor penguin in the Antarctic.

0 400 800 1200 1600 2000 km

0   400   800   1200 miles

Different views of the world

A globe

The Earth is a **globe,** round like an orange. It is very difficult to draw a map of the Earth on a flat piece of paper. If the skin is peeled off an orange in segments and laid flat, then any shapes drawn on the skin are split apart. The same happens with the globe. Mapmakers draw the world from different views, all of them change the shapes of the land. These different views are called projections.

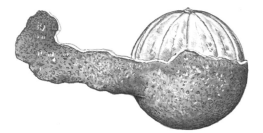
Peeling an orange

Peeling the world

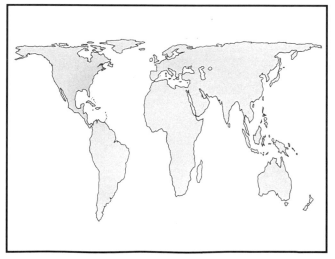
The Peter's projection (first drawn in 1977)

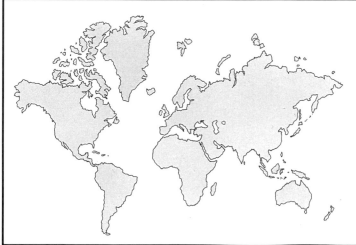
Mercator's projection (first drawn in 1569)

The best way to see the shapes of the continents and oceans is on a globe, but this is difficult to carry around. Atlases are much more handy to use. This atlas uses a spotter half globe to show where the map area is on the Earth's surface.

Glossary

Barges Flat-bottomed boats used on rivers or canals for transporting goods.

Continents The Earth's large areas of land.

Dykes Ditches and sea walls built to keep water from flooding across land.

Equator An imaginary line around the middle of the world.

Fiord A long narrow area of sea water between hills found along the coast in Norway and in other countries.

Globe A ball with a map of the world drawn on it.

Inca A person who lived in Peru, South America, many years ago.

Independent Used to describe a person, group of people, or country, who look after themselves.

Inuit A group of people who live along the Arctic coasts of North America and Greenland.

Iron ore A natural resource used to make iron.

Issues Important subjects.

Mayas A group of people who live in Central America and Southern Mexico.

Monsoon The monsoon is the wind which brings a season of very heavy rain to South-East Asia.

Muslims People who follow the religious teachings of the Prophet Muhammad.

Olympic Games A world sports competition held every four years.

Plantations Areas of farmland where, for example, cotton, sugar, tea or rubber is grown.

Prairies A huge area of grassland in North America used for growing crops.

Rainforest A natural forest in warm, wet climates. A rainforest contains many different sorts of animals and plants.

Raw materials The things used for making other goods. Sheep's wool is the raw material for making jumpers.

Resource A resource is something of value a country has, such as coal or oil, which can be used to help make the country rich.

Temperate A temperate climate is not too cold or too hot.

Vikings A group of people who lived in Scandinavia many years ago.

Index